MW01073530

Celebrating your year

1965

a very special year for

_____

_____

_____

_____

_____

A message from the author:

Welcome to the year 1965.

I trust you will enjoy this fascinating romp down memory lane.

And when you have reached the end of the book, please join me in the battle against AI generated copy-cat books and fake reviews.

Details are near the back of the book.

Best regards,
Bernard Bradforsand-Tyler.

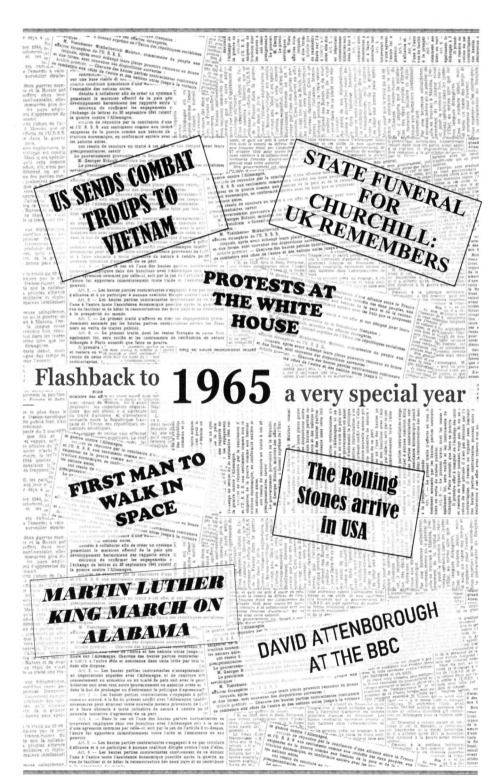

US SENDS COMBAT TROUPS TO VIETNAM

STATE FUNERAL FOR CHURCHILL: UK REMEMBERS

PROTESTS AT THE WHITE HOUSE

Flashback to **1965** a very special year

FIRST MAN TO WALK IN SPACE

The Rolling Stones arrive in USA

MARTIN LUTHER KING MARCH ON ALABAMA

DAVID ATTENBOROUGH AT THE BBC

Contents

Frameless electric cooking is a wonderful way to start your family toward the joy of total electric living. With a modern electric range, your kitchen keeps cool. Walls, cabinets and curtains stay clean longer. And, of course, only electric ovens have the exclusive new improvements that make them so easy to keep clean.

You live better electrically.

Throughout America, this Gold Medallion identifies electric homes in which families enjoy total electric living with flameless electric home heating and appliances.

Let's flashback to 1965, a very special year.

Was this the year you were born?

Was this the year you were married?

Whatever the reason, this book is a celebration of your year,

THE YEAR 1965.

Turn the pages to discover a book packed with fun-filled
fabulous facts. We look at the people, the places, the
politics and the pleasures that made 1965 unique
and helped shape the world we know today.

So get your time-travel suit on, and enjoy this trip down memory
lane, to rediscover what life was like, back in the year 1965.

Kodak brings the <u>Instamatic</u> Camera idea to movies
...and introduces a new era in movie enjoyment

Kodak has redesigned the movie camera. New Kodak Instamatic Movie Cameras load *instantly, automatically.* Just slip the Kodapak Movie Cartridge into the camera and shoot! No winding. No flipping. Zoom model shown, less than $175. Other Kodak Instamatic Movie cameras from less than $50.

Kodak has redesigned the movie film with 50% more picture area for better, more lifelike movies. The new Kodapak Movie Cartridge is factory-loaded with improved Kodachrome 11 Film in the new Super 8 format—giving you 50 feet of uninterrupted shooting.

Kodak has redesigned the movie projector. The Kodak Instamatic M70 Movie Projector lets you show any scene at normal, fast, or slow-motion speeds—forward and reverse. "Still" projection, too. Brilliant illumination, automatic threading. Less than $160. Other models from less than $65.

1965 Family Life in the USA

Imagine if time-travel was a reality, and one fine morning you wake up to find yourself flashed back in time, back to the year 1965.

What would life be like for a typical family, in a typical town, somewhere in America?

Young family celebrating a birthday, 1965.

The 1960s was a decade of change, of shifting social movements, of vibrant and vocal youth, of rebellion and rejection. Yet, what we fondly refer to as "The Sixties", really only began in the year 1965.

The first half of the decade more rightly belonged to the Post-War era, also known as the Golden Years, the era of the Baby Boomers (1946-1964).

76.4 million Americans were born during the baby boom years, accounting for 40% of our population. As the first of the baby boomers were turning 18, their views, aspirations and demands would shape America, and the world, for decades to come.

By 1965, we'd grown tired of our post-war traditional conservative family values. Our youth had discovered a new energy in the exciting movements sweeping the UK. London's Mods and the Swinging Sixties encouraged freedom of expression, liberation, and rejection of the constraints of our old-world order. The "British Invasion" conquered the world through music, art, film, and fashion.

The Rolling Stones, circa 1965.

America's youth just couldn't get enough of all things British. We had time to indulge in life's pleasures, we had money to spare.

Beatlemania, fans at Shea Stadium, 15th Aug 1965.

Sean Connery as James Bond.

During the '60s we benefited from America's longest ever period of continuous economic growth. GDP averaged 5% growth annually and peaked at around 6.5% during 1965 and 1966.

We were more likely to be working in offices, rather than tilling the land or working on assembly lines. We had more spending power than ever before. And we enjoyed an excessive consume-and-discard culture, driven by a mature advertising industry which instilled in us the belief that we constantly needed more and more, bigger and better.

But beyond pleasure-filled amusement and leisure time, we were also fighting for a better world. Students rallied against the draft, feminists demanded gender equality, African Americans marched for civil rights, professors held teach-ins, and everywhere, our citizens were standing up against US involvement in the Vietnam War.

Demonstrators outside the White House protesting police brutality against civil rights demonstrators in Selma, Alabama, 17th Apr 1965.

Martin Luther King addresses students at UCLA on civil rights, 27th Apr 1965.

Right top: Anti-Vietnam War protest, Washington, D.C. 27th Nov 1965.

Right: The first campus anti-war teach-in, organized by university professors, was held at the University of Michigan on the 24th March 1965.

New Admiral Duplex 19 fits your old refrigerator space!

Never before! A 19.1 cu. ft. freezer-refrigerator... side by side in one beautiful cabinet... just 35¾" wide, 5'4" tall! Now, the big family with a small kitchen can shop once a week!

The Admiral Duplex 19's new stand-up design and all-foam Thinwall insulation save valuable space inside and out... nearly double your present refrigerator's storage capacity.

The Duplex 19's left side is a spacious 246 lb. freezer. Everything's easy to reach. No stooping. No stretching.

The Duplex 19's right side is a roomy 12.1 cu. ft. refrigerator. Holds gallon milk bottles, tall soft drink bottles, big hams, bulky packages. Your food storage problems are over!

The Admiral Duplex is available with all-new, quality automatic ice maker and automatic defrosting in *both* freezer and refrigerator. In copper bronze, citron yellow, turquoise and white. Brushed chrome doors optional extra. Three sizes: 35¾" wide (19.1 cu. ft.); 41" wide (22 cu. ft.); 48"wide(26.5cu.ft.). *There's nothing finer at any price.*

← Only 35¼ inches wide →

Admiral Duplex 19
Newest thin-wall freezer refrigerator

New Admiral Duplex 19 fits your old refrigerator space!

Never before! A 19.1 cu. ft. freezer-refrigerator... side by side in one beautiful cabinet... just 35³/₄" wide, 5'4" tall! Now, the big family with a small kitchen can shop once a week!

The Admiral Duplex 19's new stand-up design and all-foam Thinwall insulation save valuable space inside and out... nearly double your present refrigerator's storage capacity.

The Duplex 19's left side is a spacious 246 lb. freezer. Everything's easy to reach. No stooping. No stretching.

The Duplex 19's right side is a roomy 12.1 cu. ft. refrigerator. Holds gallon milk bottles, tall soft drink bottles, big hams, bulky packages. Your food storage problems are over!

The Admiral Duplex is available with all-new, quality automatic ice maker and automatic defrosting in *both* freezer and refrigerator. In copper bronze, citron yellow, turquoise and white. Brushed chrome doors optional extra. Three sizes: 35³/₄" wide (19.1 cu. ft.); 41" wide (22 cu. ft.); 48" wide (26.5 cu. ft.). *There's nothing finer at any price.*

Now just imagine you flashed back to a town in 1965 England or Western Europe.

London's "Swinging Sixties" was now center stage for music, arts, fashion, and all things cultural.

With the ravages of war firmly in the past, the cultural revolution known as Swinging Sixties quickly became the United Kingdom's greatest export of the decade. Focused on fun-loving hedonism and rejection of traditional conservatism, this was a revolution full of excitement, freedom and hope. Unlike their American counterparts, UK's baby boomers were free of conscription and the miseries of war.

Carnaby Street, London, 1965.

Artists, musicians, writers, designers, film-makers, photographers, and all types of creatives and intellectuals descended on London. Their radical views brought about a revolution in social and sexual politics.

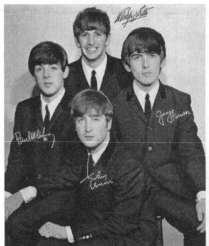

The Beatles.

Musicians led the charge with their own uniquely British sound. Influenced by American rock 'n' roll of the '50s, yet infused with innovative new sounds, their songs inspired their fans to express their individuality and freedom.

The Who, London, 1965.

The Rolling Stones, London, 1965.

Pirate radio stations brought "the London Sound" to the airwaves, pushing bands like The Rolling Stones, The Kinks, The Yardbirds, and The Who, along with early '60s mega-band The Beatles, to the top of the charts.

In fashion, designer Mary Quant created youthful styles for running, jumping and dancing in. Along with other trend-setting designers, the fashion scene centered around London's Carnaby Street and King's Road in Kensington.

London also introduced us to the first non-aristocratic looking supermodels, who soon became household names. Through magazines worldwide, they guided us on the newest trends in urban style and street wear.

Supermodels Jean Shrimpton and Twiggy, 1965.

In literature, retired British spy Jean Le Carré penned unstoppable mystery thrillers infused with cold-war espionage. He, along with crowd-pleasing British favorites like Agatha Christie, Alistair MacLean, and Victor Canning, became instant International best sellers.

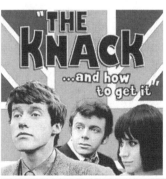

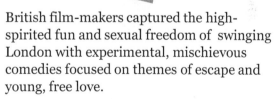

British film-makers captured the high-spirited fun and sexual freedom of swinging London with experimental, mischievous comedies focused on themes of escape and young, free love.

THE ROYAL TOUCH

For offices, schools or homes, it's the most easy-going, self-reliant, sweet-typing, money-saving, good-looking Royal family of electric, manual and portable typewriters.

Ask the girls: students, top executives' secretaries, professional women. They'll tell you they can always spot a Royal by the touch. The Royal Touch on electrics, manuals and portables is light, responsive, smooth, nimble. Uniquely so.

Behind that Royal Touch are 60 years of engineering and manufacturing experience. And a testing program that's rigid and rigorous. Before any Royal typewriter goes out into the world (whether it's the full-featured office Electress, the ruggedly dependable Empress® Manual or a sturdy Royal portable), every part and every action is tested, checked — then checked again. When you buy a Royal, you can be sure it'll have that light and easy touch... the one-and-only Royal Touch.

ROYAL® McBEE
CORPORATION

The sweet-typing Royal Touch, left to right: is on the Empress (sturdiest, most service-free manual); on the Electress (top executives' secretaries prefer it) and the Safari® Portable (with a glamorous travel case, for girls on the go).

Every year more Royal typewriters are bought in America than any other brand.

The Royal Touch. For offices, schools or homes, it's the most easy-going, self-reliant, sweet-typing, money-saving, good-looking Royal family of electric, manual and portable typewriters.

Ask the girls: students, top executives' secretaries, professional women. They'll tell you that they can always spot a Royal by the touch. The Royal Touch on electrics, manuals and portables is light, responsive, smooth, nimble. Uniquely so.

Behind that Royal Touch are 60 years of engineering and manufacturing experience. And a testing program that's rigid and rigorous. Before any Royal typewriter goes out into the world (whether it's the full-featured office Electress, the ruggedly dependable Empress Manual or a sturdy Royal portable), every part and every action is tested, checked—then checked again. When you buy a Royal, you can be sure it'll have that light and easy touch... the one-and-only Royal Touch.

Every year more Royal typewriters are bought in America than any other brand.

Swinging London was largely seen as a middle-class consumer-driven diversion, centered around the fashionable West End. Elsewhere, counter sub-cultures existed, such as the Mods and the Rockers. The groups were easily identified by their outfits and choice of vehicles, the Rockers on their motorbikes wore leather jackets, while the Mods on their mirror-decked scooters preferred Italian-cut suits.

In 1964 violent clashes between the Rockers and Mods erupted, leaving both groups branded as trouble-makers.

Throughout the decade, British families had greater purchasing power and disposable incomes. Stable economic growth led to rising living standards with excess cash to spend on leisure and amusements. Home ownership rates rose markedly as a 20-year post-war construction boom provided much needed affordable housing stock. A "job for life" was a reality, and job security made home ownership widely attainable.

Education for girls, and the growth of feminism, saw more young women entering the workforce. Although equality was still a long way off, it was now possible to be female, single, living away from home, and independent.

Try and tell yourself you don't want one. Just try. Pontiac Grand Prix
1965: The Year of the Quick Wide-Tracks

Our Love Affair with Automobiles

Our love affair with cars began way back in the early '50s, and by 1965 we were irreversibly addicted to our vehicles. Americans owned an average of 1.3 cars per family. Automobile numbers had risen 45% during the preceding ten years. Although car costs had risen markedly, so too had real wages. The cost of a standard family car was now equivalent to five months of the average family annual income.

Increased car ownership and the creation of the National Highway System gave Americans a new sense of freedom. Office commuters could live further out from city centers and commute quickly and comfortably to work.

Rush hour traffic, New York in the 1960s.

Rural areas were no longer isolated, benefiting from access to food, medical and other supplies. The suburbanization of America, which had begun in the early '50s, now saw 40% of the population living in the suburbs. The car was no longer a luxury, it was a necessity.

Catering to the suburban lifestyle, fully enclosed, air-conditioned shopping malls sprang up country-wide during the 1960s. A typical mall design saw one or two anchor stores surrounded by hundreds of smaller specialty shops, sitting within a vast expanse of carparks.

Northland Mall carpark, Columbus, Ohio, 1964.

How to buy a new Buick.
(An easier lesson than you might expect.)

Not only is owning a new Buick pleasant, it's entirely possible. What you do is this—first, you just look. Long and hard. At the styling. At the way things fit. At the interiors, with their rich fabrics and vinyls. Next, you drive. A LeSabre 400, say, like the one in our picture. Choose this one and you get a 250-hp Wildcat V-8 and that feather-smooth, Super Turbine automatic of ours. (Plot your test route past your house and watch the neighbors eat their hearts out.) And finally, you price. That should be the start of a long and beautiful friendship. Visit your Buick dealer soon. Your friendly Buick dealer.

Wouldn't you really rather have a Buick?

How to buy a new Buick.
(An easier lesson than you might expect.)

Not only is owning a new Buick pleasant, it's entirely possible. What you do is this—first, you just look. Long and hard. At the styling. At the way things fit. At the interiors, with their rich fabrics and vinyls. Next, you drive. A LeSabre 400, say, like the one in our picture. Choose this one and you get a 250-hp Wildcat V-8 and that feather-smooth, Super Turbine automatic of ours. (Plot your test route past your house and watch the neighbors eat their hearts out.) And finally, you price. That should be the start of a long and beautiful friendship. Visit your Buick dealer soon. Your friendly Buick dealer.

Wouldn't you really rather have a Buick?

Detroit was America's car manufacturing powerhouse, where "the Big Three" (Ford, General Motors and Chrysler) produced 90% of cars sold in the country. Using technological innovation, with significant financial and marketing strength, the Big Three successfully bought out or edged out all smaller competitors throughout the '50s and '60s.

1965 was the golden year of the American "muscle cars". These high-performance coupes usually came with large, powerful V-8 engines and rear wheel drive. Also known as "super cars" they were designed with drag-racing engine capability to satisfy our desire for power above all else.

1965 New Yorker Hardtop by Chrysler.

Sales, profits, and production soared in 1965 reaching all-time highs. Motor vehicle fatalities also set new records, with 47,089 car-related deaths recorded during the year.

1965 Chevelle by Chevrolet.

Ralph Nader's bestselling book, *Unsafe at Any Speed: The Designed-In Dangers of the American Automobile*, was published on 30th November 1965. The book and its author would play critical roles bringing about legislative changes to vehicle safety the following year.

Five car-producing countries dominated the industry in the first half of the decade: England, France, Germany and Italy, with America in top spot. However, starting in 1965, these mainstays would be rocked by the dramatic expansion of the Japanese automobile industry. Within two years, Japan would position itself in second place, behind only America, for total number of vehicles produced.

Japanese domestic demand had grown rapidly in the early '60s through sales of ultra-compact and affordable *kei cars*. Midsize family cars, more suited to international export, soon followed.

There's more pleasure in driving a Colt 1000

1965 Mitsubishi Colt 1000.

1965 Honda S600 convertible.

Heralding a full line of Honda automobiles
HONDA *S600*

Japanese cars were reliable, affordable, compact, efficient and popular, quickly making Toyota, Nissan, Mitsubishi, Mazda and Honda the export market leaders. 100,000 Japanese cars were exported in 1965 alone, increasing nearly 200-fold from start to end of the decade. 1965 marked the beginning of Japanese automobile world domination.

1965 Daihatsu Compagno —the first Japanese car to be sold in the UK.

Everything looks roomier, smarter, sportier...at the wheel of the new Ford XL. But only a test drive can tell you about the velvet authority of Ford's competition-bred performance. And the Ford XL is so solid, strong, precisely built that, in actual tests, an XL with V-8 and Cruise-O-Matic transmission rode quieter than a new Rolls-Royce.

Best year yet to go Ford!
Test Drive Total Performance '65

FORD

For the Action Crowd...

New RCA VICTOR Portables with Solid Copper Circuit dependability

Your new "Pick of the Portables" can *take it—wherever* you take it—because every Sportabout TV gives you RCA Solid Copper Circuits. Solid Copper Circuits replace old-fashioned "hand wiring"—eliminate over 200 possible trouble spots. RCA Victor Solid Copper Circuits won't come loose and short circuit to cause service headaches. They're the circuits of the Space Age.

You get the sharpest, clearest pictures possible with these sharp new RCA Victor Sportabouts. They "shift gears" electronically for greater picture-pulling power—a must for fringe area reception.

And remember: more people own RCA Victor than any other television, black and white or color. Shouldn't you?

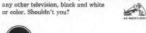 The Most Trusted Name in Electronics

RCA Victor Solid Copper Circuits are the circuits of the Space Age. They replace old-fashioned "hand wiring" in over 200 possible trouble spots . . . . for greater dependability, better performance.

For the Action Crowd...

New RCA Victor Portables with Solid Copper Circuit dependability

Your new "Pick of the Portables" can *take* it—*wherever* you take it—because every Sportabout TV gives you RCA Solid Copper Circuits. Solid Copper Circuits replace old-fashioned "hand wiring"—eliminate over 200 possible trouble spots. RCA Victor Solid Copper Circuits won't come loose and short circuit to cause service headaches. They're the circuits of the Space Age.

You get the sharpest, clearest pictures possible with these sharp new RCA Victor Sportabouts. They "shift gears" electronically for greater picture-pulling power—a must for fringe area reception.

And remember: more people own RCA Victor than any other television, black and white or color. Shouldn't you?

RCA Victor Solid Circuits are the circuits of the Space Age. They replace old-fashioned "hand wiring" in over 200 possible trouble spots...for greater dependability, better performance.

RCA   The Most Trusted Name in Electronics

Television's Race to Color

Those of us old enough will remember when black and white television was the norm. We neither questioned it nor demanded anything different. 1965, however, was color television's breakthrough year, when the three major networks sparked a race-to-color war.

By the end of the 1965-'66 season, all three networks aired their entire primetime programs in color. There remained one minor problem however—most households did not own a color TV set.

At the start of 1965, 92% of American households owned a television set (84% in the UK)[1], of which less than 5% were color. By the end of the year, 9.2% of family TVs would be in color, and by 1971 that figure would be nearly 50%.[2]

Family TV time in 1965.

Elsewhere in the world, access to color television was not nearly as widespread as in the USA. Canada received color emissions in 1966, with the UK following in 1967. Australia would wait till 1975 for their first color television broadcasts.

[1] americancentury.omeka.wlu.edu/items/show/136.
[2] tvobscurities.com/articles/color60s/.

Most Popular TV Shows of 1965

1	Bonanza	11	Green Acres
2	Gomer Pyle, U.S.M.C.	12	Get Smart
3	The Lucy Show	13	The Man from U.N.C.L.E.
4	The Red Skelton Hour	14	Daktari
5	Batman (Thurs.)	15	My Three Sons
6	The Andy Griffith Show	16	The Dick Van Dyke Show
7	Bewitched	17	Walt Disney's Wonderful World of Color
=	The Beverly Hillbillies		
9	Hogan's Heroes	=	The Ed Sullivan Show
10	Batman	19	The Lawrence Welk Show
		=	I've Got a Secret

* From the Nielsen Media Research 1965-'66 season of top-rated primetime TV series in the USA.

Musical variety programs remained popular in 1965, with westerns, dramas and kids' shows added to the mix. But sitcoms continued to pull the highest ratings, with six of the top ten programs of 1965 being situation comedies.

Lucille Ball and Vivian Vance in *The Lucy Show* (CBS. 1962-1968).

The ever-popular *Gomer Pyle, U.S.M.C.* aired for five seasons from 1964-1969. The series followed the life of the incompetent but lovable Gomer Pyle in the Marine Corps, and his overly intense Sergeant, Vince Carter.

Jim Nabors & Frank Sutton in *Gomer Pyle, U.S.M.C.* (CBS. 1964-1969).

The sitcom fantasy *Bewitched* aired for eight seasons in the '60s and continues to air today internationally as reruns.

Elizabeth Montgomery, Dick York and Agnes Moorehead in *Bewitched* (ABC. 1964-1972).

Bob Crane and John Banner in
Hogan's Heroes (CBS. 1965-1971).

Eddie Albert and Eva Gabor in
Green Acres (CBS. 1965-1971).

The television networks were quick to turn out new programs to keep us tuning in. Here are just a few of the new programs that aired for the first time in 1965: *Hogan's Heroes, Green Acres, Get Smart,* and *I Dream of Jeanie*. Other notables include *Lost in Space, Days of our Lives, The Wild Wild West, Gidget, The Dating Game, The Dean Martin Show*, and *The Thunderbirds*.

Don Adams and Barbara Feldon in
Get Smart (NBC. 1965-'69, CBS. 1969-'70).

Barbara Eden and Larry Hagman in
I Dream of Jeanie (NBC. 1965-1970).

New! SWANSON 3 Course BEEF DINNER

Complete from Soup to Dessert!

Here's the most complete frozen beef dinner ever put in a single package. First course: piping hot Campbell's Tomato Soup. Second course: lean slices of tender beef in natural beef gravy, with hashed brown potatoes and golden corn in butter sauce. For dessert: sweet 'n' tangy Cherry Crisp. Only Swanson makes 3 Course Dinners, and this new *Beef* Dinner is the latest addition. There's also Turkey, Salisbury Steak, and Fried Chicken. Try 'em next time you feel like eating a complete 3 Course Dinner.

To get more that's good **TRUST SWANSON**

Here's the most complete frozen beef dinner ever put in a single package. First course: piping hot Campbells Tomato Soup. Second course: lean slices of tender beef in natural beef gravy, with hashed brown potatoes and golden corn in butter sauce. For dessert: sweet 'n' tangy Cherry Crisp. Only Swanson makes 3 Course Dinners, and this new *Beef* Dinner is the latest addition. There's also Turkey, Salisbury Steak, and Fried Chicken. Try 'em next time you feel like eating a complete 3 Course Dinner.

The Cold War–Nuclear Arms Race

Cold War tensions between the two former allies–the USSR and the USA– continued from post war 1945 till 1991.

Starting in the USA as policies for communist containment, the distrust and misunderstanding between the two sides quickly escalated from political squabbling, to a military nuclear arms race. Trillions of dollars in military spending saw both sides stockpile their nuclear arsenals, strategically positioning and pointing their missiles closer and closer to each other.

In the early '60s the USA's global nuclear weapon stockpiles increased rapidly, peaking in 1967. By 1965, the USA had 31,140 nuclear weapons, against the Soviet's 6,130 weapons. Additionally, the UK held 440 weapons, France (32 weapons), and China (5 weapons).[1]

The Cuban Missile Crisis of 1962 saw the superpowers square off over a 13-day tense confrontation, the closest we ever came to full-scale nuclear war.

Protestors in front of Ambassador Hotel, Santo Domingo, Dominican Republic, 1965.

In April 1965, keen to avoid another such stand-off, US President Lyndon B. Johnson approved US military intervention in the Dominican Republic's escalating civil war. US troops began arriving on 28th April, just as US civilians were being evacuated.

The troops remained for one month, officially ending their involvement in September 1966.

[1] tandfonline.com/doi/pdf/10.2968/066004008.

The Cold War–Space Race

Throughout the 1960s, the Cold War dominated our lives on the ground and in the skies. Cold War tensions affected everything from our politics and education, to our interests in fashion and popular culture. During this time, the USSR achieved many firsts, putting them at a military, technological and intellectual advantage.

Sputnik 1 was the world's first artificial earth satellite, launched into orbit in 1957. Yuri Gagarin became the first human to orbit the earth in 1961, and Valentina Tereshkova became the first woman in space in 1963. On 18th March 1965, Alexei Leonov became the first human to walk in space.

The USSR continued to take the lead with longer space flights, more complex space walks and other activities.

Yuri Gagarin, first man in space.

Alexei Leonov, first person to walk in space.

Valentina Tereshkova, first woman in space.

The US responded by increasing spending on education and defense in a bid to catch up with the Soviets. NASA had been established in 1958, and in 1961, US President John F. Kennedy declared that America would land a man on the moon. The space race was on.

HAVEN'T TRIED SMIRNOFF? WHERE IN THE WORLD HAVE YOU BEEN?

You've really been out of touch if you haven't explored Smirnoff with orange juice, with tomato juice, with 7-Up® (in the new Smirnoff Mule). Or discovered that crystal clear Smirnoff makes the dryest Martinis, the smoothest drink on-the-rocks. Only Smirnoff, filtered through 14,000 pounds of activated charcoal, makes so many wonderful drinks so wonderfully well. Don't wait any longer. Let the next Smirnoff launching be yours!

Get acquainted offer! Try the delicious drinks you've been missing with this new half quart sampler bottle. Now available in most states

Always ask for ***Smirnoff*** VODKA
It leaves you breathless®

Haven't tried Smirnoff?
Where in the world have you been?

You must have been on another planet if you haven't tried smooth, flawless Smirnoff. Smirnoff is *not* like other vodkas. The unique filtration process (through 9,000 pounds of charcoal), makes Smirnoff crystal clear, remarkably free of taste or odour. Nothing less will do for your party. Smirnoff shows you *know*. Smirnoff says you *care*.

Always ask for Smirnoff vodka. It leaves you breathless.

By 1965 the US was ready to launch the first of their Project Gemini space missions. The 2-man Gemini 3 capsule launched in March 1965, demonstrating a change of orbit maneuver. Geminis 4 and 5 launched in June and August 1965, the latter spending a record eight days in space. Geminis 6A and 7 lunched in December 1965, achieving the first space rendezvous.

Gemini 3 astronauts Gus Grissom and John Young training in the space simulator.

3rd June 1965– Astronaut Ed White outside Gemini 4, becoming the first American to "spacewalk".

In 1966, an additional five Gemini missions were successfully completed. The program proved humans could fly the duration needed to reach the moon and back and perform any required tasks outside of the spacecraft.

20th July 1969– Buzz Aldrin walks on the moon. Photo by Neil Armstrong.

Pilots Neil Armstrong, James A. Lovell and Edwin "Buzz" Aldrin, of later Apollo missions, all took part in the Project Gemini missions.

The USA would achieve its goal, winning the Space Race in 1969 when Apollo 11 brought Aldrin and Armstrong to the moon for their historic lunar walk, lasting $2^1/_4$ hours.

The Cold War–Battlefield Vietnam

Fearful that a "domino effect" would see an uncontained spread of communism across the world, the US committed to supporting South Vietnam, financially and militarily, during its 30-year-long bloody civil war against North Vietnam (the Viet Cong). At the same time, communist China and USSR were jointly aiding the Viet Cong's invasion southward. Vietnam had become a Cold War battlefield.

America's involvement in the Vietnam War (known in Vietnam as the American War) drastically intensified in 1965, when President Johnson ordered hundreds of thousands of US combat forces to be sent to Vietnam.

American troops in Vietnam soared during 1965 from 23,000 to 185,000 by year's end. By 1968, more than 536,000 US troops would be fighting the Viet Cong.[1]

Compulsory draft registration of all men aged 18-26 would provide forced conscripts to meet the shortfall in volunteers.

As the war dragged on, US soldiers were beset with rising casualties, physical and psychological stress, and increasing distrust of their own government. Forced to fight a war they didn't believe in, morale among the draftees was low. Drug usage became rampant. It is estimated up to 50% of US soldiers experimented with marijuana, opium and heroin, cheaply available on the streets of Saigon. US military hospitals would later report drug abuse victims far outnumbered actual war casualties.

[1] vietnamgear.com/war1965.aspx.

Anti-Vietnam Protests

8th March– US authorities confirmed the use of chemical warfare against the Viet Cong. 20 million gallons of herbicides, including Agent Orange, were sprayed over Vietnam, Laos and Cambodia during the decade.[1] Cancers, birth defects and other serious health issues resulted.

Although most Americans supported the country's involvement in the Vietnam War, a vocal group of intellectuals, students and artists began speaking out against what they believed was an immoral war.

In early 1965, students began organizing anti-war campus teach-ins. They argued that the foreign powers had secret imperialistic intentions in Asia and should not be involved in this civil war. By the end of the year, large-scale protests were being held across the US, in Paris, London and Rome. This had grown into a global Peace Movement.

Media coverage helped expose the brutality of the war and the true number of casualties. The Peace Movement was boosted by those opposed to the draft, which drew unfairly from the minorities and the less wealthy. African Americans, religious leaders, veterans, soldiers and parents also joined.

[1] history.com/topics/vietnam-war/agent-orange-1.

"Bloody Sunday" Alabama Riots

By the time Martin Luther King Jnr. arrived in Alabama in January 1965, racial tensions were at a tipping point. Having been granted the right to vote, with the passing of the Civil Rights Act of 1964, African Americans in many states found themselves continuously blocked from registration. Alabama was extreme, with blacks representing more than half of the population, yet only 2% of registered voters.[1]

Over a series of state-wide peaceful protests, demonstrators found themselves being arrested by the thousands. And on 25th February, activist Jimmie Lee Jackson died from a state trooper gunshot wound received days earlier. His death hastened the planning of a series of bigger and longer protest marches to follow.

"Bloody Sunday"– On 7th March, the first march attempt started peacefully, soon running into a wall of awaiting state troopers. The brutal attack which followed was televised nationally. Among the injured were organizers John Lewis,[2] who suffered a skull fracture, and Amelia Boynton, who was beaten unconscious.

"Turnaround Tuesday"– Hundreds of clergymen joined the second march attempt on 9th March. King led a crowd of 2500 to the site of Sunday's attack where they knelt to pray. Obeying a court restraining order, the crowd returned to Selma.

[1] history.com/news/selma-bloody-sunday-attack-civil-rights-movement.
[2] John Lewis, one of the original 13 Freedom Riders of 1961, was a life-long civil rights leader and politician. He was one of six organizers for the 1963 March on Washington. In 1965 he led the first of the Selma to Montgomery marches. From1987-2020, Lewis served 17 terms in the US House of Representatives (Democratic Party).

On 21st March, protected by hundreds of federal guardsmen and FBI agents, the demonstrators began their 54-mile walk. Five days later over 25,000 marched into Montgomery.

On 6th August, President Johnson signed the Voting Rights Act of 1965. It was a landmark piece of US federal legislation prohibiting racial discrimination in voting.

Civil rights demonstrators walk from Selma to Montgomery, 21st -25th March 1965.

15th March, Harlem, New York– Outrage at the brutality of the Bloody Sunday march sparked protests in many cities nationwide.

Sir Winston Churchill (born 30th Nov 1874) passed away in his London home on 24th January 1965. His state funeral, in planning since 1953, would be the largest in history, making him the first civilian to receive the honour normally reserved for kings and queens. Attended by the Queen and representatives from over 100 nations, including 6 monarchs, 6 presidents and 16 prime ministers, the event was broadcast live on the BBC and seen by an estimated 350 million people (one-tenth of the world's population).[1]

The event started with the chimes of Big Ben and the roar of 90 canon shots from nearby Hyde Park. More than a million people lined the route from Westminster to St. Paul's Cathedral. The lead-lined coffin, draped in a flag and resting on a gun carriage, was escorted by members of the Royal Navy and other military units.

Churchill was Prime Minister from 1940-1945 and 1951-1955. He led the Conservative Party for 15 years (having led the Liberal Party for 20 years earlier).

Churchill was a writer and politician. He had served as an army officer and war correspondent in the British India, Anglo-Sudan and Second Boer Wars. He received a Nobel Prize for Literature in 1953.

Churchill is remembered as a great war-time leader.

[1] history.com/news/winston-churchills-funeral-50-years-ago.

Political Upheaval in Southeast Asia

During 1965, the Southeast Asian nations of Singapore, Indonesia and the Philippines would inaugurate new presidents, changing their social and economic directions for the decades to come.

Singapore separated from the Malaysian Federation on 9th August 1965. Led by Prime Minister Lee Kuan Yew, this tiny city state would transform itself within a few decades, from third-world poverty into a global economic giant. Singapore is now a stable, vibrant, wealthy financial and shipping hub, which prides itself on security and multi-racial harmony.

With low levels of corruption, Singapore consistently ranks highly on several international indicators: GDP per capita, education, healthcare, safety, housing, life-expectancy, and quality of life to name a few.

In October 1965, the fragile democracy of Indonesia fell into a violent power struggle between the government's Presidential Guard and the Indonesian Army. An estimated half million people died in executions and social unrest that followed. General Suharto gained control by military coup, appointing himself as acting president. The authoritarian regime of President Suharto would rule until 1998.

President Ferdinand Marcos was elected president of the Philippines in December 1965. He would declare martial law in 1972, holding onto power until 1986. During this time he silenced the media, the opposition and regular citizens. Rampant corruption placed the country under extreme poverty and crushing debt. In 1986 he fled with his family to Hawaii. It is estimated the Marcos family stole US$5-10 billion during his rule.

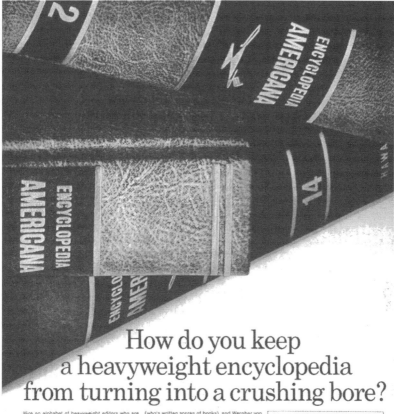
How do you keep a heavyweight encyclopedia from turning into a crushing bore?

Hire an alphabet of heavyweight editors who are very easily bored. At least that's how we do it. We've got BAs, MAs, LLDs, and PhDs editing our Encyclopedia Americana. And almost every last one of them, back in his own brilliant study days, did his sleeping in dull lecture classes. People like that just plain don't have the patience to edit volumes of dry facts and leaden explanations. They want experts whose writing wakes them up. Teachers who make their pages teach. Authorities who know as much about writing as they do about theirs subjects.

So our editors hunt and sift. And read. And yawn. And turn their noses up. Until they find us biochemists like Isaac Asimov. (He writes like a novelist because he is also a novelist.) Physicists like George Gamow. (You may have read his "One, Two, Three Infinity".) Space scientists like Willy Ley (who's written scores of books, and Wernher von Braun (who wrote a book with Ley). Psychologists like Arnold Gesell (whose books have changed the thinking of American Parents). These men are first-rate writers as well as first-rate scientists. Read any one of their entries in the Americana. Even if the subject doesn't interest you, we think the writing will. And you won't have to be a scientist to understand it. We get the same kind of writing from our writer-economists, writer-musicologists, writer-historians...Together they've made the Americana more than a heavyweight encyclopedia. They've packed a lively university between the covers of its thirty fat, juicy volumes. We promise you, though the Americana may weigh heavy on your shelves, it will never weigh heavy upon your spirits.

1965 in Cinema and Film

Max von Sydow as Jesus in *The Greatest Story Ever Told* (United Artists, 1965).

The early '60s in cinema was memorable for many sweeping heroic period films such as *Spartacus* (1960), *Lawrence of Arabia* (1962) and *Cleopatra* (1963). However, with the biblical epic *The Greatest Story Ever Told* (April 1965), and the romantic classic *Doctor Zhivago* (Dec 1965), the era of big budget epic movies would come to an end. Movie studios could no longer sustain the financial burden required by these extravaganzas.

Cinema attendance had been declining for more than a decade as movie theaters competed directly with television for the viewing audience.

Omar Sharif and Julie Christie in *Doctor Zhivago* (MGM. 1965).

Highest Paid Stars

1 Sean Connery
2 John Wayne
3 Doris Day
4 Julie Andrews
5 Jack Lemmon
6 Elvis Presley
7 Cary Grant
8 James Stewart
9 Elizabeth Taylor
10 Richard Burton

1965 film debuts

Woody Allen	What's New Pussycat
Sonny & Cher	Wild on the Beach
Robert De Niro	Encounter
Michael Gambon	Othello
Philip Kaufman	director–Goldstein
George Lucas	director–Look at Life

* From en.wikipedia.org/wiki/1965_in_film.

Clint Eastwood as The Man with No Name in *For a Few Dollars More* (United Artists, 1965).

To reduce production costs the major studios looked to filming in cheaper locations elsewhere, in particular Britain, Spain and Italy. This was the era of the modern "Spaghetti Westerns"– Italian-made productions starring a host of European actors with fading, or up-and-coming Hollywood stars. Clint Eastwood transitioned from television to cinema with three such films: *A Fistful of Dollars* (1964), *For a Few Dollars More* (1965), and *The Good, The Bad and The Ugly* (1966).

Hollywood also had to compete with rising talent from foreign film directors and foreign stars, such as Brigitte Bardot (France), Sophia Loren (Italy), Sean Connery and Richard Burton (England).

Brigitte Bardot. Sophia Loren.

Top Grossing Films of the Year

1	The Sound of Music	20th Century Fox	$138,700,000
2	Doctor Zhivago	MGM	$112,100,000
3	Thunderball	United Artists	$63,600,000
4	Those Magnificent Men in their Flying Machines	20th Century Fox	$31,100,000
5	That Darn Cat!	Disney	$28,100,000
6	The Great Race	Warner Bros.	$25,300,000
7	Cat Ballou	Columbia	$20,700,000
8	What's New Pussycat?	United Artists	$18,800,000
9	Shenandoah	Universal	$17,300,000
10	Von Ryan's Express	20th Century Fox	$17,100,000

* From en.wikipedia.org/wiki/1965_in_film by box office gross in the USA.

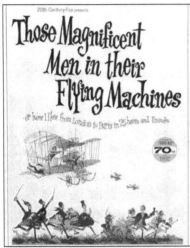

David Lean's three hour long epic romantic drama *Doctor Zhivago*, filmed in the UK, earned mixed reviews upon release. Starring Omar Sharif and Julie Christie, the movie would win five Oscars at the Academy Awards, missing out on Best Picture to *The Sound of Music*.

The Sound of Music

One of Hollywood's most loved and commercially successful musicals, *The Sound of Music* (20th Century Fox) reached #1 at the box office within its first month of release. It would go on to break box office records in 29 countries, becoming the highest grossing film of all time.

The movie would win a total of eleven film industry awards, including five Academy Awards.

Based on the 1959 stage musical by Rogers and Hammerstein, the plot loosely depicts the real-life memoir of Maria, and the singing Family von Trapp as they flee Nazi occupied Austria.

Light-hearted and joyful, *The Sound of Music* continues to delight us through film and theatre reruns. Around 50,000 tourists join guided tours to visit film locations in Salzburg every year.

Kym Karath, Debbie Turner, Angela Cartwright, Duane Chase, Heather Menzies, Nicholas Hammond, Charmian Carr, Julie Andrews and Christopher Plummer as *Sound of Music's* Family von Trapp.

The Sound of Music was the first American movie to be completely dubbed in a foreign language. Dubbed versions were released in Europe and Japan, with subtitles for other languages.

Beach Blanket Bingo (American Intl, 1965). *How to Stuff a Wild Bikini* (Amer Intl, 1965).

Aimed at a younger carefree audience, the "beach party film" genre of the mid-'60s centered around surfing, bikinis and parties, with original songs and music throughout. Focused on having a good time, these films often lacked parental characters, ignoring adult concerns and problems.

Wild on the Beach (20th Century Fox, 1965).

Dr. Goldfoot and the Bikini Machine (American International, 1965).

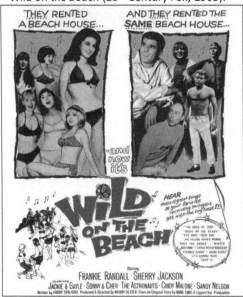

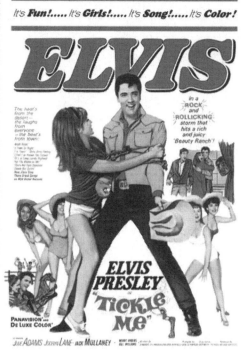

Harum Scarum (MGM. 1965).　　　　　*Tickle Me* (Allied Artists Pictures, 1965).

Girl Happy (MGM. 1965).

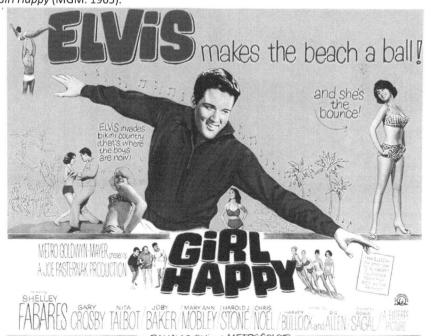

The British Invasion Concert Posters

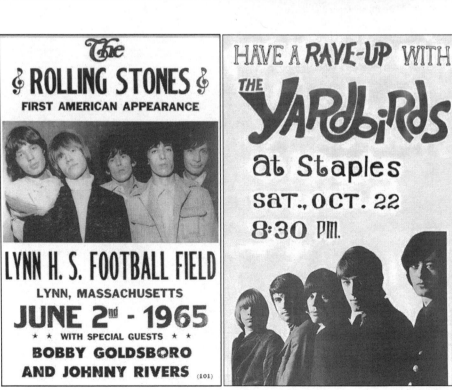

Why is Western Electric so proud of this old sewing machine when we're really in the telephone business?

Because it still works. A Connecticut housewife still relies on it. When Western Electric sold it to her mother in 1918, we backed it with a solid five-year guarantee which, of course, expired unnoticed. Even in those days, reliability was a matter of prime importance to Western Electric.

We haven't sold electrical appliances like sewing machines for more than a generation because we concentrate on our main business—providing Bell telephones and other equipment that makes them serve the public so well. And our standards for reliability are even higher today. Take your Bell telephone for example. How long has it been since it needed repair—if ever?

Even though our experience in communications goes back ninety-six years, our job as manufacturing and supply unit of the Bell System gets tougher each year. Unlike a sewing machine, your Bell telephone is interconnected to millions of others. This requires a nationwide network of literally billions of parts. Every part of it—down to the tiniest component—must be made to work dependably—each with each as one unified system.

So you see why we're so strict about quality. It's one of the ways we help your Bell telephone company bring you efficient, dependable communications services at low cost.

He got his Stereo Sound Center.

She got her walnut sideboard.

And Porta-Fi gives them **both** music in any room.

He got his Stereo Sound Center. She got her walnut sideboard. And Porta-Fi gives them both music in any room.

Without adding one new wire!

That's the unique home-entertainment innovation available from only G.E.

Here's how Porta-Fi works. An optional transmitter in the console sends sound through your house wiring. The Porta-Fi speaker plays it, wherever you plug it in. Or you can shut off the console sound and listen to Porta-Fi alone.

There's more, much more! A 4-track, 2-channel tape deck with twin dynamic microphones, AM/FM/FM-Stereo Tuner, superb Tonal-1 record changer, and the G-E Man Made diamond stylus.

The eight balanced speakers are front mounted in acoustically lined, closed chambers. And there's a list of extras as long as your arm.

Choose from 38 other models. Stereo consoles and stereo-television combinations priced from under $150 to over $1000. Most with Porta-Fi option, a number with tape, too. At your G-E dealer's.

Musical Memories

By 1965, the youth of the world were clamoring for all things British. The Beatles-led "British Invasion" delivered a stream of British talent, pushing their music to the top of the charts. Of the twenty-seven records to hit #1 on the US charts, thirteen were from the UK.

British bands were touring in record numbers, including the Yardbirds, The Who, Herman's Hermits, The Kinks and The Rolling Stones. On 15th August, The Beatles performed the first stadium concert in the history of rock, playing to 55,600 fans at Shea Stadium in New York.

The Beatles inspired other artists to write their own songs, play their own music, and experiment with exotic sounds. Indian instruments, feedback and distortion, spiced with a dose of marijuana and LSD, paved the way for psychedelic pop and rock of the late '60s.

Motown brought soul music to the mainstream with a string of five consecutive US #1 hits. In March '65, The Supremes, Stevie Wonder, Smokey Robinson & The Miracles, Martha & The Vandellas, and others, toured 20 UK cities. As Motown was largely unknown, concert attendance remained pitiful. Motown's UK popularity soon skyrocketed after Dusty Springfield hosted the Motown acts on national TV's popular *Ready Steady Go!* music show.

28th Apr– Luciano Pavarotti made his debut at La Scala, Milan, in Franco Zeffirelli's production of *La Bohème*.

25th Jul– Bob Dylan performed at the Newport Folk Festival using an electric guitar, marking the beginnings of the folk-rock genre. An artist ahead of his time, he was booed by the crowd.

1965 Billboard Top 30 Songs

	Artist	Song Title
1	Sam the Sham & the Pharaohs	Wooly Bully
2	Four Tops	I Can't Help Myself (Sugar Pie Honey Bunch)
3	The Rolling Stones	(I Can't Get No) Satisfaction
4	We Five	You Were on My Mind
5	The Righteous Brothers	You've Lost That Lovin' Feelin'
6	Petula Clark	Downtown
7	The Beatles	Help!
8	Herman's Hermits	Can't You Hear My Heartbeat
9	Elvis Presley	Crying in the Chapel
10	The Temptations	My Girl

The Four Tops, 1968.

Petula Clark.

The Temptations, 1968.

Elvis Presley, 1958.

	Artist	Song Title
11	The Beach Boys	Help Me, Rhonda
12	Roger Miller	King of the Road
13	Jewel Akens	The Birds and the Bees
14	Mel Carter	Hold Me, Thrill Me, Kiss Me
15	Junior Walker & the All Stars	Shotgun
16	Sonny & Cher	I Got You Babe
17	Gary Lewis & the Playboys	This Diamond Ring
18	Ramsey Lewis Trio	The 'In' Crowd
19	Herman's Hermits	Mrs. Brown, You've Got a Lovely Daughter
20	The Supremes	Stop! In the Name of Love

The Beach Boys, 1965.

Sonny and Cher, 1966.

21	The Righteous Brothers	Unchained Melody
22	Herman's Hermits	Silhouettes
23	The Seekers	I'll Never Find Another You
24	Jay and the Americans	Cara Mia
25	The Byrds	Mr. Tambourine Man
26	Sounds Orchestral	Cast Your Fate to the Wind
27	Barbara Mason	Yes, I'm Ready
28	Tom Jones	What's New Pussycat?
29	Barry McGuire	Eve of Destruction
30	The McCoys	Hang On Sloopy

* From the *Billboard* top 30 singles of 1965.

Fashion choices from the Montgomery Ward catalog, Summer 1965.

Fashion Trends of the 1960s

The 1960s was an exciting decade for fashion, with new trends that caught on and transformed quickly. It was a decade of fashion extremes driven by shifting social movements, radical youth, rebelliousness and rejection of traditions.

In the early '60s, fashion was content to continue the conservative classic style of the previous decade. The elegant sheath dress and tailored skirt-suits were favored for day wear.

And for dinners and cocktails, '50s style hourglass dresses were still common. Skirts stayed long, full and very lady-like. Matching accessories such as gloves, hat, scarves, jewelry and stiletto or kitten-heel shoes were mandatory.

Jacqueline Kennedy may have been the US first lady for only three years, but as first lady of fashion, her iconic status has endured till this day. Always impeccably groomed, her every move was analyzed and cataloged by newspaper and style magazines for every lady to follow.

Here are some of her classic iconic looks:

- Tailored skirt-suit with three-quarter sleeve length box jacket and matching pill box hat.
- Sheath dress with white gloves and low-heel pump shoes.
- A-line dress, long or short, with three-quarter length gloves for evening.

However, the conservative elegance of the early '60s would soon be energetically and wholeheartedly rejected. The decade of the 1960s belonged to the British youth centered around London, who would capture the world's attention with their free spirits, energy, music, and style. By 1967, the "British Invasion" had exploded on the world, introducing us to the "Mods" and the "Swinging Sixties". These movements defined the era and changed the world of fashion forever.

The Mods were clean-cut college boys who favored slim-fitting suits or short jackets over turtle-neck or buttoned up polo shirts. Pants were pipe-legged with no cuffs, worn over pointed polished shoes or ankle boots.

The Mods were obsessed with Italian fashion, French haircuts, alternative music and Vespa scooters.

Mod fashion was adopted by the many British Invasion bands of the mid-'60s: The Kinks, The Who, The Yardbirds, The Rolling Stones and The Beatles all adopted the Mod look in the early part of their careers.

For the girls, London designer Mary Quant created fashion for the young and free-spirited woman. Credited for inventing the mini-skirt, Quant considered her youthful designs liberating, allowing women to run and move freely. Her clients were hedonistic, creative, wealthy, and sexually liberated. They helped shape the Swinging Sixties cultural revolution.

Quant's Kings Road boutique featured her trademark simple short sheath dresses in bold or floral patterns, worn with solid colored or patterned tights.

She also championed trousers for women– with choices ranging from long flared, harem, or ankle length Capris, to mid-length Bermudas and skimpy hotpants.

Below Left: Mary Quant.
Below Right: Models in Quant plastic coats and boots.

Top: Models wear Mary Quant dresses.
Above: Quant inspired street dresses.

Quant's experimental use of new materials was revolutionary. Shiny PVC raincoats came in an array of solid statement colors, matched with patent vinyl boots. Synthetic dresses paired with a range of bold, colorful plastic jewellery, handbags and accessories.

The Swinging Sixties was also the era of the first wave of British supermodels–tall, skinny, leggy young ladies who broke with the aristocratic look of earlier-generation models. With enormous eyes and quirky descriptive names, Jean Shrimpton, Twiggy and Penelope Tree were in-demand icons world-wide.

Penelope Tree for *Vogue,* October 1967.

Twiggy for *Italian Vogue*, July 1967.

Twiggy various photo shoots.

Jean Shrimpton for *Vogue*, Sept 1967.

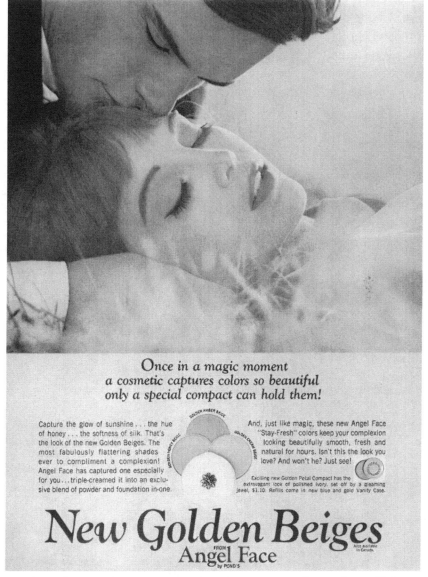

Once in a magic moment a cosmetic captures colors so beautiful only a special compact can hold them!

Capture the glow of sunshine... the hue of honey... the softness of silk. That's the look of the new Golden Beiges. The most fabulously flattering shades ever to compliment a complexion! Angel Face has captured one especially for you... triple-creamed it into an exclusive blend of powder and foundation in-one.

And just like magic, these new Angel Face "Stay-Fresh" colors keep your complexion looking beautifully smooth, fresh and natural for hours. Isn't this the look you love? And won't he? Just see!

Exciting new Golden Petal Compact has the extravagant look of polished ivory, set off by a gleaming jewel, $1.10. Refills come in new blue and gold Vanity Case.

Known as the Space Age designer, French couturier André Courrèges employed geometric shapes in metallic silvers and stark whites to give his dresses futuristic forms. His revolutionary designs from the mid-'60s mixed plastics and fur with leathers and wool, accessorising with astronaut inspired helmets, goggles and flat white go-go boots.

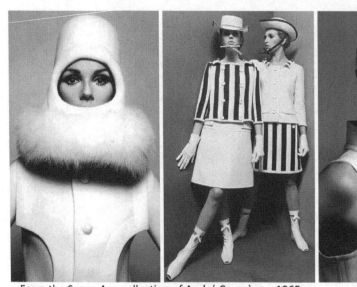 

From the Space Age collection of André Courrèges, 1965.

André Courrèges' cut out dress.

Inspired by Courrèges, Space Bride by Jezebel, 1966 New York.

As the fashion and attitudes of swinging London spread to America and other parts of the world, the subculture became commercialized on a mass scale and began to loose its vitality. The fun loving movement morphed into the psychedelic rock and early hippie movements.

Led by musicians such as The Beatles, The Beach Boys, Pink Floyd and The Who, and fuelled by widespread use of marijuana and LSD, psychedelic fashion became an expression of the hallucinogenic experience. Bright colors, swirling patterns and kaleidoscopic floral designs adorned full flowing forms in soft fabrics.

Photo from The Beatles *Magical Mystery Tour,* 1967.

The psychedelic rock movement petered out by the end of the 1960s, but the hippie generation was only just beginning. Hippies would drive fashion forward, well into the next decade.

New Dec-La-Tay* plunges in front.
Dips low in back.
Straps stretch smoothly over
shoulders. French blue,
nude, pink, black and white.
A, B, C cups, 5.00.
*Reg. U. S. Pat. Off. ©1964
by Maidenform, Inc., makers of bras, girdles,
active sportswear.

I dreamed
Paris
was at
my feet...
in my
maidenform
bra

I dreamed Paris was at my feet... in my Maidenform bra

New Dec-La-Tay plunges in front.
Dips low in back.
Straps stretch smoothly over shoulders. French blue, nude, pink, black and white.
A, B, C cups, 5.00.

Also in Sports

2nd Jan– Joe Namath signed a contract with the New York Jets "that made him the richest rookie in the history of pro football–and probably any other sport."[1] The deal reportedly earned him $400,000 over three years, the highest amount for any athlete in any sport to date.

2nd Mar– The Australian Swimming Union banned Olympic champion Dawn Fraser for 10 years for alleged misconduct during the 1964 Tokyo Olympics. Fraser had angered the Union by marching in the opening ceremony and wearing an older more comfortable swimming costume without permission.

18th Apr– In golf, Jack Nicklaus won the US PGA Masters Tournament. He would go on to win 18 major championships over the next 21 years, making him one of the greatest golfers of all time.

4th May– Baseball's Willie Mays hit his 512th career home run for the San Francisco Giants, taking the National League record for home runs. He hit over 50 home runs in 1965, a feat he had earlier accomplished in 1955. Mays was NL Most Valuable Player twice, in 1965 and a decade earlier in 1954.

25th May– reigning heavyweight champion Cassius Clay (later Muhammad Ali) defended his title against former champion Sonny Liston. The rematch lasted less than 2 minutes. Clay TKO Liston midway through the first round, with a difficult-to-see "phantom punch".

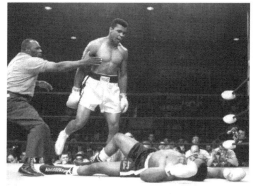

19th-25th Jul– The first All-African Games were held in Brazzaville, Congo. 250 athletes from 30 countries competed in the Olympic style multi-sport events. Now known as the African Games, the event is held every four years with 54 Nations competing.

[1] *Associated Press* Newspaper 3rd Jan 1965.

Mary Allen Wilkes–World's First Home PC

In 1965, 28-year-old Mary Allen Wilkes became the first person in the world to work from home on a personal computer. Working remotely from Baltimore, Wilkes can be seen here at her home office, in the living room of her parent's house.

Wilkes at her
home computer, 1965.

Long before smart phones, tablets and laptops were invented, the first modern computers existed as giant machines, occupying large sealed airconditioned rooms, requiring towers of punch cards to program and numerous people to operate.

Wilkes joined Massachusetts Institute of Technology (MIT) as a programmer just as work was beginning on the Laboratory Instrument Computer (LINC) in the early '60s. Their goal was to create a real-time interactive computer operated by a single user—now known as the personal computer.

Wilkes in front of a LINC at M.I.T. in 1963.

In order to continue working on the LINC, Wilkes followed her colleagues as they left MIT to join Washington State University in St. Louis. However, reluctant to move from Baltimore, she arranged to work remotely from the living room of her parent's home. She was tasked to develop and program the user-computer interface.

In the '70s Wilkes left computing to study law. She would practice as a trial lawyer for many years and teach law at Harvard Law School for many decades.

Science and Medicine

3rd Apr– The world's first space nuclear power reactor, SNAP-10A, was launched by the USA. It operated for 43 days.

6th Apr– The first commercial communications satellite, Intelsat 1, was launched. It would provide television, telephone and facsimile transmission between North America and Europe for four years.

11th May– The first carousel slide projector was patented by David E. Hansen, an engineer at the Eastman Kodak Company.

27th Jul– US President Johnson signed a bill requiring cigarette packets to display a warning about the health dangers of smoking.

 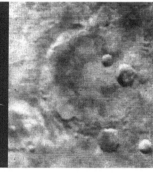

14th Jul– US spacecraft Mariner 4 flew by Mars, becoming the first spacecraft to return images from the Red Planet.

Kevlar, a strong, lightweight, heat-resistant material, was invented by Stephanie Kwolek for DuPont. Kevlar has become the main ingredient in armored vests, tanks and tires. It is five times stronger than steel.

Evidence of cosmic microwave background, confirming the Big Bang Theory of the Universe, was discovered by two separate teams in the US. Their papers were published in the Astrophysical Journal in 1965.

The world's first portable defibrillator was invented in Belfast, Ireland, by Professor Frank Pantridge. Using car batteries for the current, it was installed in an ambulance.

Try something different for a change...
Turn to Salem for a taste that's Springtime fresh
Rich tobacco taste • Menthol soft flavor
Try Salem filter cigarettes.

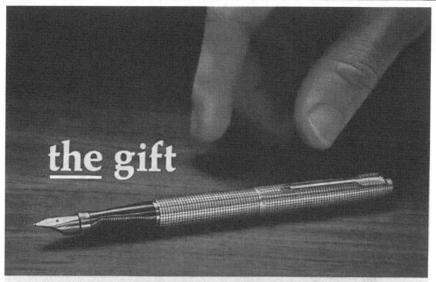

The new Parker 75...in solid sterling silver

The Parker 75 is the first personal-fit pen, tailored to write his own way. It costs $25.

The Parker 75 is a gift both personal and memorable. No other gift can be so completely custom-fitted to its owner.

The beautifully sculptured grip nests his fingers in its curvatures. There is less pressure as he writes; his fingers do not tire. The point can be adjusted to the exact angle at which he writes—his hand stays relaxed. The angle is set by a dial as carefully calibrated as the lens on a $400 camera. The 75 is precision throughout.

The grace and beauty of his writing is enhanced by the cushion flexing of the 14K gold point. Point sizes are available for all writing styles from broad, bold strokes to Spencerian tracery.

He chooses the filling method he prefers. The parker 75 fills cleanly with a large-capacity cartridge or, with the handy converter, it fills from an ink bottle.

The case of the Parker 75 is sterling silver, deep-engraved and subtly antiqued.

We urge you to see the Parker 75 at better department stores, jewelry, pen, or stationery stores. It is worth seeing.

Other News from 1965

1st Jan– Indonesia withdrew from the United Nations in protest at the presence of Malaysia with which it was engaged in a guerrilla war.

4th Mar– David Attenborough became the new controller of BBC2, expanding the fledgling channel with a diverse mix of programs including arts and natural history.

11th Apr– An estimated 50 tornadoes, known as Palm Sunday tornadoes, tore through 6 midwest US states, killing around 250 people and injuring an additional 1500 people.

10th May– Warren Buffett took control of Berkshire-Hathaway, a failing textile business which he later closed, keeping only the name for his future company.

25th May– India and Pakistan engaged in border fights resulting in thousands of casualties on both sides. Skirmishes continued, escalating in August, before a formal ceasefire was signed on 22nd September 1965.

1st Jun– A devastating cyclone killed 35,000 people along the Ganges River, East Pakistan. A similar cyclone had occurred one month earlier.

22nd Jun– Japan signed a peace treaty with South Korea agreeing to $500 million in compensation for wartime excesses and for South Korean women used as sex slaves during the Japanese occupation.

30th Jul– US President Lyndon B. Johnson signed the Social Security Act of 1965 into law, providing additional Medicare and Medicaid benefits to people aged 65 or over.

6th Aug– US President Lyndon B. Johnson signed the Voting Rights Act of 1965, outlawing literacy tests and other discriminatory voting practices that disenfranchised the African American population.

9th Sep– Hurricane Betsy tore through Louisiana, New Orleans, resulting in 76 deaths and $1.4 billion in damage. New Orleans would not suffer another major hurricane till Hurricane Katrina 40 years later.

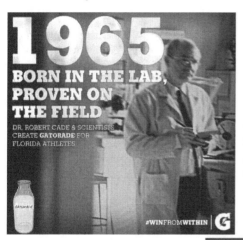

9th Sep– A research team at the University of Florida created a new energy-enhancing drink for athletes. The drink was originally invented for the university's athletics team–the Gators. They would call the drink Gatorade.

25th Sep– The *Tom & Jerry* cartoon series made its TV debut on CBS as heavily edited versions of the 161 short films which aired from 1940 till 1967. Criticized for being racist, the black character of Mammy Two Shoes was replaced with a chubby Irish woman.

9th Nov– The Great Northeast Blackout left all of New York State, parts of seven neighboring states, plus eastern Canada, in total darkness when the entire Northeastern transmission network failed.

Famous People Born in 1965

13th Jan– Bill Bailey,
British comedian.

1st Feb– Princess
Stéphanie of Monaco.

7th Feb– Chris Rock,
American stand-up comedian.

18th Feb– Dr. Dre [Andre
Romelle Young], American
rapper & record producer.

23rd Feb– Helena Suková,
Czech tennis player (14
Grand Slam titles).

23rd Feb– Kristin Davis,
American actress.

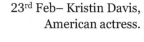

23rd Feb– Michael Dell,
American computer
manufacturer.

25th Mar– Sarah Jessica
Parker, American actress.

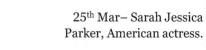

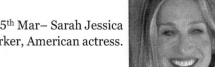

30th Mar– Piers Morgan,
English newspaper editor
& TV personality.

4th Apr– Robert Downey Jr,
American actor.

3rd May– Rob Brydon,
British actor & comedian.

10th May– Linda Evangelista, Canadian supermodel.

31st May– Brooke Shields, American model & actress.

7th Jun– Damien Hirst, English artist.

10th Jun– Elizabeth Hurley, English actress.

7th Jul– Jeremy Kyle, English radio & television presenter.

23rd Jul– Slash [Saul Hudson], English-American rock guitarist & songwriter.

31st Jul– J. K. Rowling, English writer.

1st Aug– Sam Mendes, British stage & film director.

11th Aug– Viola Davis, American actress.

19th Aug– Kyra Sedgwick, American actress.

28th Aug– Shania Twain, Canadian singer.

3rd Sep– Charlie Sheen, [Carlos Estévez], American actor.

23rd Sep– Mark Woodforde, Australian tennis player & broadcaster.

14th Sep– Dmitry Medvedev, Russian President then Prime Minister (2008-'20).

27th Sep– Steve Kerr, American basketball guard & coach.

8th Oct– Matt Biondi, American swimmer.

2nd Nov– Shah Rukh Khan, Indian actor, producer & TV personality.

21st Nov– Bjork, Icelandic singer.

30th Nov– Ben Stiller, American actor.

30th Nov– Prince Akishino of Japan.

3rd Dec– Katarina Witt, German figure skater.

31st Dec– Gong Li, Chinese actress.

Who's drinking all that Diet-Rite Cola?

Everybody!

Dad, mother, sister, too. Everyone in the family is drinking Diet-Rite Cola now because it is by far the best-tasting cola of all. Better than old-time favorites... or their low-calorie offshoots. No sugar at all. Less than 1 calorie per bottle. Far and away America's favorite low-calorie cola. Just the thing for your family, too.

diet-rite cola
America's no.1 low-calorie cola

Who's drinking all that Diet-Rite Cola?

Everybody!

Dad, mother, sister, too. Everybody in the family is drinking Diet-Rite Cola now because it is by far the best-tasting cola of all. Better than old-time favorites... or their low-calorie offshoots. No sugar at all. Less than 1 calorie per bottle. Far and away America's favorite low-calorie cola. Just the thing for your family, too.

Diet-rite cola   America's no.1 low-calorie cola

Census Statistics [1]

- Population of the world   3.34 billion
- Population in the United States   199.73 million
- Population in the United Kingdom   54.24 million
- Population in Canada   19.63 million
- Population in Australia   11.31 million
- Average age for marriage of women   20.6 years old
- Average age for marriage of men   22.8 years old
- Average family income USA $6,900 per year
- Minimum wage USA $1.25 per hour

Costs of Goods [2]

- Average home $20,367
- Average new car $2,650
- Cadillac de Ville $5,430
- A gallon of gasoline $0.30
- Cambells soup $0.89 for 6 cans
- A loaf of bread $0.21
- A gallon of milk $0.95
- Rump steak $1.49 per pound
- Spare ribs $0.49 per pound
- Veal cutlets $0.68 per pound
- Fresh eggs $0.53 per dozen
- Sugar $0.38 for 5 pounds
- Beer $0.99 for a 6-pack
- A can of hair spray $0.47

[1] Figures from worldometers.info/world-population, US National Center for Health Statistics, Divorce and Divorce Rates US (cdc.gov/nchs/data/series/sr_21/sr21_029.pdf) and US Census Bureau, Historical Marital Status Tables (census.gov/data/tables/time-series/demo/families/marital.html).
[2] Figures from thepeoplehistory.com, mclib.info/reference/local-history and dqydj.com/historical-home-prices/.

Use our handy time machine.
(It'll put extra days in your vacation.)

Use our handy time machine.
(It'll put extra days in your vacation.)

Vacations are always too short.

But if you want to add days to yours, go by Boing jet and spend the whole time there.

Leave in the evening of your last working day. At 600 miles and hour, you can be practically anywhere in the country that very night.

You not only get a head start on your vacation–you also make life easier for yourself. No long, hard drives. No searching for places to eat of sleep. No over-tired children. Instead, after a few delightful hours aboard a Boeing jet, you're there.

And you can enjoy every last minute of vacation. Stay until the sun sets Sunday. Whiz back by Boeing jet at ten miles a minute.

Plan now. Let a Boeing time machine turn your next two-week vacation into 16 days of pleasure for the whole family!

The franc is local currency in Tahiti. So is this.

Papeete, Palermo or Pittsburgh–wherever you go, your Bank of America Travelers Cheques get a big welcome. Because they're backed by the world's largest bank–with a money-back guarantee against loss or theft. When you travel, carry money only you can spend–Bank of America Travelers Cheques.

These words first appeared in print in the year 1965.

MACROBIOTIC

wiggle room

convenience store

flashcube

Lava Lamp

granny flat

Focus group

megabyte

beta-blocker

MIDLIFE CRISIS

GRUNGE

pixel

avian influenza

jet lag

BIOHAZARD

TALK SHOW

POP ART

* From merriam-webster.com/time-traveler/1965.

A heartfelt plea from the author:

I sincerely hope you enjoyed reading this book and that it brought back many fond memories from the past.

Success as an author has become increasingly difficult with the proliferation of **AI generated** copycat books by unscrupulous sellers. They are clever enough to escape copyright action and use dark web tactics to secure paid-for **fake reviews**, something I would never do.

Hence I would like to ask you—I plead with you—the reader, to leave a star rating or review on Amazon. This helps make my book discoverable for new readers, and helps me to compete fairly against the devious copycats.

If this book was a gift to you, you can leave stars or a review on your own Amazon account, or you can ask the gift-giver or a family member to do this on your behalf.

I have enjoyed researching and writing this book for you and would greatly appreciate your feedback.

Best regards,
Bernard Bradforsand-Tyler.

Please leave a
book review/rating at:

https://bit.ly/1965-reviews

Or scan the QR code:

Flashback books make the perfect gift- see the full range at

https://bit.ly/FlashbackSeries

Image Attributions

Photographs and images used in this book are reproduced courtesy of the following:

Page 6 – From *Life* mag, 2nd Apr 1965. Source: books.google.com/books?id=6IIEAAAAMBAJ&printsec. (PD image).*
Page 8 – From *Newsweek* 9th Aug 1965. Source: flickr.com/photos/91591049@N00/14773074891/ by SenseiAlan. Attribution 4.0 International (CC BY 4.0).
Page 9 – Image by Edison Electric Institute, from *Life* magazine, 8th Jan 1965. Source: books.google.com/books?id=yEgEAAAAMBAJ&printsec. (PD image).*
Page 10 – Rolling Stones in 1965, source: guitarnoise.com/lessons/play-with-fire/. Creator unknown. – Fans at Shea Stadium, source: vintag.es/2016/03/1965-shea-stadium-beatles-biggest.html. Pre-1978, no copyright mark (PD image). – Connery, source: flickr.com/photos/slightlyterrific/5380276160 by kate gabrielle. Attribution 4.0 International (CC BY 4.0).
Page 11 – White House demonstration, source: loc.gov/item/2014645538/ courtesy of the Library of Congress (PD image). – MLK address, source: newsroom.ucla.edu/stories/archivist-finds-long-lost-recording-of-martin-luther-king-jr-s-speech-at-ucla. Pre-1978, no copyright mark (PD image). – Peace marchers, source: pritzkermilitary.org/explore/museum/digital-collection/view/oclc/ 879575630 courtesy of the Pritzker Military Museum and Library (PD image). – Campus sit-in, pre-1978, no copyright mark (PD image).
Page 12 – From *Life* mag, 12th Mar 1965. Source: books.google.com/books?id=JkEEAAAAMBAJ&printsec. (PD image).*
Page 13 – Carnaby Street, London UK, photo from 1965. Unknown source. Pre-1978, no copyright mark (PD image).
Page 14 – The Beatles signed photo, source: freeclassicimages.com/images/beatles_autograph.jpg. – The Who by KRLA Beat/Beat Publications, Inc. Source: commons.wikimedia.org/wiki/File:The_Who_in_1965.png. – The Rolling Stones, source: en.wikipedia.org /wiki/File:Stones_ad_1965-2.jpg. – Quant dresses, source: nationaalarchief.nl/onderzoeken/ zoeken?activeTab=photo_legacy&qf_f_Webwinkel=Ja&qf_f_WebwinkelLabel=Ja%20(0)&searchTerm=mary%20quant. All images pre-1978, no copyright mark (PD image).
Pages 15– Shrimpton, source: search.aol.com/aol/image;_ylt=AwrT4R.VDDZfcdQAiEdjCWVH?q=jean+shrimpton. – Twiggy source: search.aol.com/aol/image;_ylt=Awr9DWs_DzZf1qwAvCtjCWVH?q=twiggy&imgl=fsuc&fr2=p%3As%2Cv%3Ai. Pre-1978, no copyright mark (PD images). – *The Whip Hand* by Victor Canning and *The Looking Glass War* by John Le Carre, book covers.** – Film posters for *The Knack and How to Get it*, by United Artists,** *The Beatles Help!* by United Artists,** and *Darling* by Embassy Pictures.**
Page 16 – From *Life* mag, 22nd Jan 1965. Source: books.google.com/books?id=x0gEAAAAMBAJ&printsec. (PD image).*
Page 17 – Rockers, Mods and group photo. Photographers unknown. Pre-1978, no copyright mark (PD image).
Page 18 – Source: flickr.com/photos/autohistorian/48943989191/ by Alden Jewell. Attribution 4.0 Int (CC BY 4.0).
Page 19 – Traffic photos from the '60s, from private unknown sources. Pre-1978, no copyright mark (PD image).
Page 20 – From *Life* mag, 22nd Jan 1965. Source: books.google.com/books?id=x0gEAAAAMBAJ&printsec. (PD image).*
Page 21 – 1965 Buick Riviera from *Life* magazine advertisement, 15th Jan 1965. Source: books.google.com/books?id=tUgEAAAAMBAJ&printsec (PD image).* – Chevelle by Chevrolet print mag advert, source: eBay (PD image).* – 1965 *Unsafe at Any Speed* book cover,** source: wikivisually.com/wiki/File:Unsafeatanyspeedcover.jpg.
Page 22 – Car images, advertisements from the '60s, unknown sources. Pre-1978, no copyright mark (PD image).
Page 23 – From *Life* mag 26th Mar 1965. Source: books.google.com/books?id=U0AEAAAAMBAJ&printsec (PD image).*
Page 24 – From *Life* mag 30th Apr 1965. Source: books.google.com/books?id=UVMEAAAAMBAJ&printsec (PD image).*
Page 25 – From Magnavox advertisement, source: imgur.com/gallery/C2E0x. (PD image).*
Page 26 – Screen still from *The Lucy Show,* 7th Jan 1963, by Desilu Productions.** Source: commons.wikimedia.org/wiki/File:Vivian_Vance_Lucille_Ball_The_Lucy_Show_1963.jpg – Publicity photo for *Gomer Pyle, U.S.M.C.* 1966, by CBS Television. Source: commons.wikimedia.org/wiki/File:Jim_Nabors_Frank_Sutton_Gomer_Pyle_1966.JPG (PD image). – *Bewitched* photo 1964, by Ashmont Productions. Source: ar.m.wikipedia.org/wiki/:ملف‎Bewitched_cast_1964.jpg (PD image).
Page 27 – *Hogan's Heroes* studio photo by CBS Television, 1st July 1966. Source: commons.wikimedia.org/wiki/File:Bob_Crane_John_Banner _ Hogan%27s_Heroes_1966.jpg. – *Green Acres* studio photo by CBS Television. Source: clickamericana.com/media/television-shows/green-acres-theme-song-lyrics-1965-1971. – *Get Smart* studio photo by CBS Television. Source: en.wikipedia.org/wiki/Don_Adams#/media/File:DonAdams.jpg. – *I Dream of Jeannie* by NBC Television. Source: commons.wikimedia.org/wiki/File:I_dream_of_jeanne_eden_hagman.JPG. All images this page pre-1978. No copyright marks (PD image).
Page 28 – From *Life* mag 26th Feb 1965. Source: books.google.com/books?id=KEEEAAAAMBAJ&printsec (PD image).*
Page 29 – From *Life* mag 23rd Apr 1965. Source: books.google.com/books?id=S1MEAAAAMBAJ&printsec (PD image).*
Page 30 – Protesters photo by Jack Lartz, U.S. Information Agency. 306-DR-48-32A. Source: archives.gov/research/foreign-policy/cold-war/conference/natanson-017.html (PD image).
Page 31 – Gagarin source: tass.com/society/899827 by Valentin Cheredintsev. – Tereshkova, source: cultura. biografieonline.it/la-prima-donna-nello-spazio/. – Leonov, source: cultura.biografieonline.it/riferimenti/unione-sovietica/. All pre-1978. No copyright marks (PD images).

Page 32 – From 1966. Source: vintageadbrowser.com/alcohol-ads-1960s/18. Pre-1978, no copyright
Page 33 – Gemini 3, 4 and Apollo 11 archival images courtesy of nasa.gov/multimedia/imagegallery. (All PD images).
Page 34 – Members of the 2nd Battalion, 14th Infantry Regiment, South Vietnam 1966. Image by James K. F. Dung, SFC, photographer, courtesy of the National Archives and Records Administration Identifier (NAID) 530610. Source: en.wikipedia.org/ wiki/Bell_UH-1_Iroquois#/media/File:UH-1D_helicopters_in_Vietnam_1966.jpg (PD image). – Anti-tank vehicles on Chu Lai beach, June 1965, archival image courtesy of the US Dept of State prev. USIA. (PD image).
Page 35 – USAF A-37 light attack aircraft by US Air Force, source: nationalmuseum.af.mil/Visit/Museum-Exhibits/Fact-Sheets/ Display/Article/196023/hitting-sanctuaries-cambodia/. – Protests sources: wallpaperswide.com/war_protest-wallpapers.html. – texashillcountry.com/life-lyndon-b-johnson-nutshell/. – peacehistory-usfp.org/vietnam-war/. All pre-1978. No copyright marks (PD images).
Page 36 – Bloody Sunday: en.wikipedia.org/wiki/Selma_to_Montgomery_marches#/media/File:Bloody_Sunday-Alabama_ police_ attack.jpeg – Turnaround Tuesday, source: books.google.com/books?id=JUEEAAAAMBAJ&printsec. (All PD images).
Page 37 – Alabama marchers, source: commons.wikimedia.org/wiki/File:Selma_to_Montgomery_Marches.jpg from the United States Library of Congress's Prints and Photographs division under the digital ID cph.3c33090 (PD image). – Harlem marchers, source: commons.wikimedia.org/wiki/File:We_March_With_Selma_cph.3c35695.jpg from the United States Library of Congress's Prints and Photographs division under the digital ID cph.3c35695 (PD image).
Page 38 – Advertisement by Bell System from 1965, source unknown. Pre-1978, no copyright mark (PD image).
Page 39 – Winston Churchill's funeral procession, 30th Jan 1965. Photograph by the official photographer of the UK Government. Source: commons.wikimedia.org/wiki/File:Churchill%27s_funeral_1965.jpg. Pre 1970 (PD image). – Churchill portrait, source: en.wikipedia.org/wiki/Winston_Churchill#/media/File:Sir_Winston_Churchill_-_19086236948.jpg by Yousuf Karsh for Library and Archives Canada, e010751643 (PD image).
Page 40 – Singapore, source: pikist.com/free-photo-vztro. – Suharto, source: en.wikipedia.org/wiki/Suharto#/media/File:President _Suharto,_1998.png. – Marcos, source: commons.wikimedia.org/wiki/File:Ferdinand-Marcos-speech.jpg. All pre-1978. No copyright marks (PD images).
Page 41 – From Life mag 26th Feb 1965. Source: books.google.com/books?id=KEEEAAAAMBAJ&printsec (PD image).*
Page 42 – Cropped still image from The Greatest Story Ever Told by United Artists.** Source: imdb.com/title/tt0059245/ mediaviewer/rm791119104. – Cropped still image from Doctor Zhivago by Metro-Goldwyn-Mayer.** Source: commons.wikimedia. org/wiki/File: Trailer-Doctor_Zhivago-Yuri_Zhivago_and_Lara.JPG.
Page 43 – Cropped still image from For a Few Dollars More by Produzioni Europee Associati / United Artists.** Source: unrealitymag.com/evolution-of-clint-eastwood-in-movies/. – Bridgitte Bardot, source: flickr.com/photos/classicvintage/ 9274563680. Attribution 4.0 International (CC BY 4.0). – Sophia Loren, source: commons.wikimedia.org/wiki/Category:Sophia_Loren_in_1962. Pre-1978 no mark (PD image).
Page 44 – Those Magnificent Men in their Flying Machines movie poster, 1965, by 20th Century Fox.** Source: en.wikipedia.org/wiki/ Those_Magnificent_Men_in_their_Flying_Machines. – The Great Race movie poster, 1965 by Warner Brothers.** Source: en.wikipedia.org/wiki/The_Great_Race. – Doctor Zhivago movie poster, 1965, by MGM.** Source: en.wikipedia.org/wiki/Doctor_ Zhivago_(film).
Page 45 – Still images and poster from the film The Sound of Music by Twentieth Century-Fox, 1965.**
Page 46 – Beach Blanket Bingo movie poster, 1965, by American International.** Source: en.wikipedia.org/wiki/ Beach_ Blanket_Bingo. – How to Stuff a Wild Bikini movie poster, 1965, by American International Pictures.** Source: en.wikipedia.org/wiki/How_to_Stuff_a _Wild_Bikini. – Dr. Goldfoot and the Bikini Machine movie poster, 1965, by American International Pictures.** Source: en.wikipedia. org/wiki/Dr._Goldfoot_and_the_Bikini_Machine. – Wild on the Beach movie poster, 1965, by Twentieth Century Fox.** Source: en.wikipedia.org/wiki/Wild_on_the_Beach.
Page 47 – Harum Scarum movie poster, 1965, by Metro-Goldwyn-Mayer.** Source: en.wikipedia.org/wiki/Harum_ Scarum_(film). – Tickle Me movie poster, 1965, by Allied Artists Pictures.** Source: en.wikipedia.org/wiki/Tickle_Me. – Girl Happy movie poster, 1965, by Metro-Goldwyn-Mayer.** Source: en.wikipedia.org/wiki/Girl_Happy.
Page 48 – Posters** for: The Beatles, Hollywood Bowl 29th Aug 1965. – The Kinks, Starlight Room, Boston, 20th March 1965. – The Rolling Stones, Lynn, Massachusetts, 2nd June 1965. – The Yardbirds at Staples, 22nd Oct 1965.
Page 49 – From Life Mag, 3rd Sept 1965. Source: books.google.com/books?id=nVIEAAAAMBAJ&printsec. (PD image).*
Page 50 – General Electric Porta-Fi Stereo print advert, source: eBay. Pre-1978, no copyright mark (PD image).*
Page 51 – The Beatles, image by EMI, Billboard p15 1st May 1965, source: en.wikipedia.org/wiki/List_of_songs_recorded_by_the_Beatles#/media/File:Beatles_ad_1965_just_the_beatles_crop.jpg. Pre-1978, no copyright mark (PD image). – Pavarotti as a young man. Source: jornada.com.mx/2010/12/27/cultura/a06n1cul. Pre-1978, no copyright (PD image). – Dylan, source: imgur.com/gallery/hCJ18, by orgeezuz, original creator unknown. Pre-1978 (PD image).
Page 52 – The Four Tops, source: commons.wikimedia.org/wiki/File:Grand_Gala_du_Disque_._The_Four_Tops,_Bestanddeelnr_921-1506.jpg 8th March 1968, by Ron Kroon / Anefo, from the Nationaal Archief, Dutch National Archives (PD image). – Petula Clarke from Les Plus Grands Succès De Petula Clark, by Sony.** – The Temptations, image from Billboard 11th May 1968 p7 by Motown Records. Source: commons.wikimedia.org/wiki/File:The_Temptations_1968.JPG. (PD image). – Elvis Presley, 1st June 1958, source: commons.wikimedia.org/wiki/File:Elvis_Presley_1958.jpg. (PD image).
Page 53 – The Beach Boys, by Capitol Records from 11th Sept 1965 Billboard advertisement p73. Source: commons.Wikimedia.org/wiki/File:The_Beach_Boys_(1965).png. Pre-1978, no copyright (PD image). – Sonny and Cher in Holland, 1st Sept 1966. Photo by Joop van Bilsen (ANEFO) from the Nationaal Archief NL. (PD image).
Page 54 – Posters** for: Sonny and Cher at the Troy Armory, N.Y. 21st Nov 1965. – Tina Turner at the Cinnamon Cinder, Calif. 18th Aug 1965. – The Supremes at the Lincoln Center, 15th Oct 1965 from the Library of Congress, by Eula, Joe, artist. Source: loc.gov/item/93503152/. – The Beach Boys at Dillon Stadium, Connecticut, 25th June 1965.
Page 55 – From Road & Track magazine, February 1965. Source: flickr.com/photos/91591049@N00/13737497015 by SenseiAlan. Attribution 4.0 International (CC BY 4.0)
Page 56 – Source: Montgomery Ward catalog, Summer 1965. Pre-1978, no copyright mark (PD image).

Page 57 – Models in office attire and tea dresses, early '50s. Creators unknown. Pre-1978, no copyright mark (PD image). – Jacqueline Kennedy on the steps of the Elysee Palace, France, 31st May 1961. From the JFK Library. Source: commons.wikimedia.org/wiki/File:President_De_Gaulle_stands_between_President_Kennedy_and_Mrs._Kennedy_o n_the_steps_of_the_Elysee_Palace.jpg (PD image). – Jacqueline Kennedy in India, 1962. Source: flickr.com/photos/ usembassynewdelhi/6914524677 by U.S. Embassy New Delhi. Attribution-(CC BY-ND 4.0). – Jacqueline Kennedy at the White House 11th May '62. Source:zh.m.wikipedia.org/wiki/File:JBKJFKMalraux.jpg. US Government photo (PD image).
Page 58 – Mod fashions, source: vintag.es/2016/07/mod-fashion-characteristic-of-british.html. Pre-1978, (PD images).
Page 59 – Models wearing Mary Quant mini dresses, creator unknown. Source: thedabbler.co.uk/2012/10/granny-takes-a-trip-back-in-time/. Pre-1978, no copyright mark (PD image). – London street scene, creator unknown. Source: vintag.es/2016/07/mod-fashion-characteristic-of-british.html. Pre-1978, no copyright mark (PD image). – Mary Quant, 16th Dec 1966. Source: commons.wikimedia.org/wiki/File:Mary_Quant_in_a_minidress_(1966).jpg by Jac. de Nijs / Anefo from the Dutch National Archives. License: Creative Commons Attribution-Share Alike 3.0 Netherlands. – Models wearing Mary Quant plastic raincoats and boots, creator unknown. Pre-1978, no copyright mark (PD image).
Page 60 – Penelope Tree, photographer Richard Avedon for *Vogue* Oct 1967. – Jean Shrimpton for *Vogue* September 1967, Twiggy for *Italian Vogue*, July 1967, and various photo of Twiggy, dates, photographers, source unknown. Images reproduced this page under terms of Fair Use are used sparingly for information only, are significant to the article created and are rendered in low resolution to avoid piracy. It is believed that these images will not in any way limit the ability of the copyright owners to sell their product.
Page 61 – From *Life* mag 2nd Apr 1965. Source: books.google.com/books?id=6lIEAAAAMBAJ&printsec (PD* image).
Page 62 – André Courrèges fur trimmed hat, creator unknown, source: alchetron.com/André-Courrèges. – Striped suits and slit glasses, creator unknown, source: vivavintageclothing.com/blog/a-salute-to-space-age-1960s-designer-andres-courreges/. – Cutout dress, photographed by William Laxton. Source: artlyst.com/news/andre-courreges-french-fashion-designer-painter-and-sculptor-dies-at-92/. – Space Bride by Jezebel, NY 1966. Images this page may be copyrighted by the creator. They are reproduced under fair use terms and rendered in low resolution to avoid piracy. It is believed these images will not in any way limit the ability of the copyright owner to market or sell their product.
Page 63 – Models wearing fashions from the late '60s. Photographers unknown. Pre-1978, (PD images). – The Beatles. Source: commons.wikimedia.org/wiki/File:The_Beatles_magical_mystery_tour_(cropped).jpg. Attribution-(CC BY 3.0).
Page 64 – From *Life* mag 26th Feb 1965. Source: books.google.com/books?id=KEEEAAAAMBAJ&printsec (PD image).*
Page 65 – Willy Mays, source: en.wikipedia.org/wiki/Willie_Mays. Pre-1978, no copyright renewal (PD image). – Cassius Clay clocking Liston in the first round 25th May 1965 with ref Joe Walcott looking on. Source: flickr.com/photos/hmk/27172391360 AP photo by H. Michael Karshis. Attribution 4.0 International (CC BY 4.0).
Page 66 – Wilkes at home in 1965, source: en.wikipedia.org/wiki/Mary_Allen_Wilkes. CC BY-SA 4.0 (PD image). – At the LIN, source: nytimes.com/2019/03/29/us/forgotten-womens-history.html?action by Joseph C. Towler, Jr. (PD image).
Page 67 – Kodak Carousel 700 Slide Projector Original Instruction Manual, 1965. – Mariner 4, source: nasa.gov/directorates/heo/ scan/images/history/November1964.html. – Mars photo by Mariner 4, source: astrobiology.nasa.gov/missions/mariner-4/. Images courtesy of NASA are in the public domain.
Page 68 – From *Life* mag 3rd Sep 1965. Source: books.google.com.sg/books?id=nVIEAAAAMBAJ&printsec (PD image).*
Page 69 – Parker Pen print advertisement, source: eBay (PD image).*
Page 70 – Palm Sunday double tornado in Indiana, source: en.wikipedia.org/wiki/1965_Palm_Sunday_tornado_ outbreak by Paul Huffman for National Oceanic and Atmospheric Administration. (PD image). – Warren Buffet, 1966, creator unknown. Source: joshuakennon.com/warren-buffetts-12-billion-disney-mistake/. Pre-1978, no copyright mark (PD image).
Page 71 – Gatorade, source unknown. Pre-1978, no copyright mark (PD image). – Tom and Jerry by Hanna Barbera.**
Page 72-74 – All photos are, where possible, CC BY 2.0 or PD images made available by the creator for free use including commercial use. Where commercial use photos are unavailable, photos are included here for information only under U.S. fair use laws due to: 1- images are low resolution copies; 2- images do not devalue the ability of the copyright holders to profit from the original works in any way; 3- Images are too small to be used to make illegal copies for use in another book; 4- The images are relevant to the article created.
Page 75 – From *Life* Mag, 16th Apr 1965. Source: books.google.com/books?id=RIMEAAAAMBAJ&printsec (PD image).*
Page 78 – Boeing Jet print advertisement, source: eBay (PD image).*
Page 79 – Bank of America Travelers Cheques print advertisement, source: eBay (PD image).*

First printed in 2020 in the USA (ISBN 979-8678330154).
2nd Ed 2021 (978-0645062366), 3rd Ed 2024 (978-1922676337).
Self-published by B. Bradforsand-Tyler.

Made in the USA
Middletown, DE
10 March 2025